WELCOME TO THE FAMILY!

Understanding Your New Relationship to God and Others

EvanTell

Foreword by R. Larry Moyer

kregel
RESOURCES

Grand Rapids, MI 49501

Welcome to the Family: Understanding Your New Relationship to God and Others

Copyright © 1996 by EvanTell, Inc.

Published by Kregel Publications, a division of Kregel, Inc., P.O. Box 2607, Grand Rapids, MI 49501.

Cover photo: Superstock

Library of Congress Cataloging-in-Publication Data
    Welcome to the family: understanding your new relationship to God and others / EvanTell, Inc.
        p.   cm.
    1. Christian life. I. Moyer, R. Larry (Richard Larry)
BV4501.2.W4175   1996   248.4—dc20   96-25499
                                                            CIP
ISBN 978-0-8254-3176-0

Printed in the United States of America

9 10 11 12 / 11 10 09 08

Contents

How Do I Maintain a Close Relationship with Christ?

How Do I Share Christ with Others?

Foreword

While traveling around the United States and the world as an evangelistic speaker, I have discovered something extremely interesting. I have met literally thousands of people who have said, "I am sorry I did not come to Christ earlier in my life." I have never met a single individual who said, "I am sorry I came to Christ."

It is not hard to understand why. Once you've come to Christ, He adds years to your life and life to your years. He adds years to your life because for the first time ever, you know beyond any doubt that you are going to be in the presence of the King forever—the most exciting life a person can know. At the same time, He adds life to your years—He gives you a reason to get out of bed in the morning and face the day with a smile because of the meaning and purpose He has brought into your life. Jesus Christ summed it up well when He said, "The thief comes only to steal, and kill, and destroy; I came that they might have life, and might have it abundantly" (John 10:10).

For that reason, it is not only good to hear you've come to Christ, it is thrilling! Welcome to the family! Through this booklet we want to help you grow in Christ and experience all the spiritual riches of being related to Him.

I am indebted to my good friend and brother in Christ Cam Abell for all his time and work in putting together this helpful material for us. His gift for and attention to detail have made this booklet available to you.

As you read and study these truths, may God cause you to "grow in the grace and knowledge of our Lord and Savior Jesus Christ" (2 Peter 3:18). Once more, "Welcome to the family!"

R. Larry Moyer

Introduction

Welcome to the family of God! You have embarked on the most exciting journey you could ever imagine!

When you trusted Christ as your Savior, you *entered* into a relationship with Christ that culminates in eternal life in heaven; *growing* in your relationship with Christ brings a full, meaningful, and purposeful life here on earth.

You can only appreciate the blessings of what God wants for you by letting God speak to you through the Bible (also called the Scriptures). The Bible consists of sixty-six separate books: thirty-nine in the Old Testament and twenty-seven in the New Testament. The Old Testament prepares for the coming of Jesus Christ; the New Testament tells of His life, ministry, teaching, final conquest, and reign.

In this study, we will focus on the books of the New Testament, which can be divided into these categories:

Christ's life and ministry	Matthew, Mark, Luke, John
Christ's early church	Acts
Christ's instructions to the church	Romans through Jude
Christ's judgment and final rule	Revelation

The Bible has been divided using chapter and verse numbers. For example, John 5:24 refers to John, chapter 5, verse 24. The books of the New Testament will be listed in the table of contents of your Bible. You will want to look up the Scripture references when they are mentioned in these studies.

How Do I Know I'm Going to Heaven?

Is it really possible that your sins are forgiven and you're on your way to heaven? Can you really know for sure that you have eternal life? Many people who profess faith in Christ would say "Maybe I'm going to heaven" or "I hope I'm going to heaven" or even "I think I'm going to heaven, but I don't know for sure."

God doesn't want you to live in such uncertainty. He wants you to *know* that you are going to heaven. A review of what God says to those who have put their trust in Christ alone as their Savior will help you to determine with certainty where you are in your relationship with Christ. Let's use a simple approach to explain some key portions of the Bible that will help you understand what has happened in your life.

The Bad News

1. "For all have sinned and fall short of the glory of God" (Rom. 3:23).

   Are you a sinner? ___ Yes ___ No

   Why? _____

   _____

When the Bible says that you and I have sinned, it means that we lie, we lust, we hate, we murder, etc. The word *sin* in the Bible actually means "to miss the mark." In other words, God is perfect and we aren't.

Suppose each of us picked up a rock, and I said to you, "We'll throw our rocks and try to hit the North Pole." Well, you might throw farther than I, or I might throw farther than you. But neither of us would hit the North Pole. We would both fall short. When the Bible says, ". . . all have sinned and fall short of the glory of God," it means that God has set a standard. That standard is God Himself. A holy God has requirements for a relationship with Him that none of us can meet. We need to be holy as He is holy, perfect as He is perfect. It doesn't matter how religiously we live, how good we are, or how hard we work; we cannot meet that standard. All of us have sinned and fall short of the glory of God.

According to this verse, you are a sinner. But the bad news is going to get worse!

2. "For the wages of sin is death . . ." (Rom. 6:23).

According to this verse, what is the result or consequence of sin in our lives?

_____

Suppose you worked for me for one day and I paid you fifty dollars. Fifty dollars would be your wages. That's what you've earned. The Bible is saying that because you and I have sinned, we have earned death. We are going to die and be eternally separated from God.

According to this verse, *the penalty for sin is death.* Since there was no way you could come to God, the Bible says that God decided to come to you. That's where the good news comes in!

The Good News

1. "But God demonstrates His own love toward us, in that while we were yet sinners, Christ died for us" (Rom. 5:8).

What was our condition when Christ died for us?

_____

What is God's attitude toward us, even though we are sinners?

_____

Let's say that you were in the hospital dying of cancer. I could come to you and say, "I want to do something for you. We'll take the cancer cells from your body and put them into my body." What would happen to me? (Think about it.) I would die. What would happen to you? (Again, think about it.) You would live. Why? Because I took the thing that was causing your death and placed it upon myself, and I died as your substitute.

The Bible says that Christ came into the world, and He took the penalty for sin that was causing your death. He placed it upon Himself, and He actually died in your place. He was your substitute. The third day, He rose to prove His claims to be God were true; He rose to prove that sin, death, and the Devil had been conquered.

According to this verse, even though you are a sinner deserving of death, *Christ died for you.* Now, just as the bad news got worse, the good news is going to get better.

2. "For by grace you have been saved through faith; and that not of yourselves, it is the gift of God; not as a result of works, that no one should boast" (Eph. 2:8–9).

On the basis of these verses, how does God ask you to respond if you want to escape the penalty of eternal punishment and receive eternal life?

_____

_____

The word *grace* means "undeserved or unmerited favor." *Saved* means to be "rescued or delivered from the penalty of sin." Now you may be wondering, What is faith? The word *faith* means "trust." For example, you weren't here when that chair you're sitting on was made, and you didn't examine how it was built before you sat on it. You are simply trusting the chair to hold you. Putting your faith in Christ means trusting Him to save you—not trusting your church membership, your good life, or your baptism to get you to heaven but trusting Christ and Him alone. Your trust has to be in the one who died for you and rose from the dead. It is then that God gives you heaven as a free gift.

In other words, according to these verses, you can be saved (rescued from the penalty of sin) *through faith in Christ and what He has done for you on the cross.*

Let's look at two more sections of the Bible that will help you know where you are in your relationship with God.

Can We Be Sure?

1. "Truly, truly, I say to you, he who *hears* My word, and *believes* Him who sent Me, *has* eternal life, and *does not come* into judgment, but *has passed* out of death into life" (John 5:24).

   Carefully examine the verbs (or action words) by answering the following questions:

   a. "he who hears My word"

      Have you heard what God has said about offering you eternal life through faith in Christ?

      ___ Yes   ___ No

   b. "and believes Him who sent Me"

      Did you believe what God said and trust Christ alone as your Savior?

      ___ Yes   ___ No

c. "has eternal life"

Does that mean later or right now?

___ Later   ___ Right now

d. "and does not come into judgment"

Does that say "does not" or "might not"?

___ Does not   ___ Might not

e. "but has passed out of death into life"

Does that say "shall pass" or "has passed"?

___ Shall pass   ___ Has passed

2. "And the witness is this, that God has given us eternal life, and this life is in His Son. He who has the Son has the life; he who does not have the Son of God does not have the life. These things I have written to you who believe in the name of the Son of God, in order that you may know that you have eternal life" (1 John 5:11–13).

Carefully answer the following questions about eternal life in these verses.

a. In verse 11, what has God given us?

_____

b. Where is eternal life found?

_____

c. Who has eternal life?

_____

d. Who does not have eternal life?

_____

e. "These things I have written to you who believe in the name
   of the Son of God, in order that you may *think* that you
   have eternal life" (1 John 5:13). Did I quote that correctly?
   Why or why not?

_____

God says that you can be sure of eternal life! You don't have to
"hope so" or "think so," but you can *know* you're on your way
to heaven.

What If I'm Still Struggling?

There are several reasons why new Christians struggle in their spiritual life. Let's look at three:

1. New Christians may confuse the *one* condition for entering
   the Christian life with *many* factors involved in *living* the
   Christian life.
       You enter the Christian life at *one* point in time—when
   you trust Christ alone as the one who died and rose again
   to pay for your sin. At that point you received the free gift
   of eternal life and you are on your way to heaven. Everything you do from that point on involves learning how to
   live the Christian life. God wants you to get to know Him
   better and grow in a way that enables you to honor God
   and enjoy the benefits of a growing relationship with Christ.

2. New Christians may struggle because they confuse the *reason*
   for living a good life.
       God does not ask a non-Christian to live a good life in order
   to get to heaven; He asks a Christian to live a good life because
   he or she is *already going* to heaven. Once you place your trust
   in Christ, God wants your life to be characterized by good works
   as a *thank you* for what He has given you. This is exactly what
   Ephesians 2:10 says:

> For we are His workmanship, created in Christ Jesus
> for good works, which God prepared beforehand, that
> we should walk in them.

3. New Christians may forget that it takes *time* and *effort* to grow as a Christian. The changes God wants to bring about in your life that will enable you to enjoy the Christian life come more slowly for some people than others. Give God time to work in your life and tell you how to grow.

If you understand this better than you have before, and you have never trusted Christ as your Savior, you need to trust Christ alone to save you.

Here's a prayer you can use to express to God that you're trusting Christ. Please understand that saying a prayer has never saved anyone. *Prayer is only the means by which you tell God that you are trusting Jesus Christ as your Savior.*

> Dear God, I know that I am a sinner. Nothing that I am or do makes me deserving of heaven. I believe Jesus Christ died for me and rose from the grave. Right now I trust Jesus Christ alone as my Savior. I am not trusting in my good life, my best efforts, my baptism, or my church membership to take me to heaven. I am trusting Christ alone to save me. Thank you for the forgiveness and everlasting life I now have. Help me to live a life from this day forward that says "thank you" for what You have just given me. In Jesus' name. Amen.

How can I make this assurance a part of my life? Two final suggestions will help.

1. Memorize the verses found in John 5:24 and 1 John 5:11–13 and review them once a day for several weeks. When the first thoughts of doubt about your relationship with Christ enter your mind, focus your attention on these verses. Assurance is based on fact, not feeling.

2. Begin to tell others what God has done for you through Christ. Tell two people what has happened in your life before the end of the day. It will help confirm in your mind what has happened in you life.

Conclusion

The verses you have looked at in this section indicate that you can know for sure that you're going to heaven *if* you've come to God as a sinner and trusted what Christ has done for you on the cross. Some mornings when you get out of bed you may not "feel" God's presence like you do on other mornings.

When you fail to obey God, Satan may cause you to doubt the sincerity of your decision. Don't make faith harder than it is; simple trust in Christ as your only way to heaven *guarantees* you eternal life. When you place your trust in Christ, who paid for your sins to give you eternal life, you have come to know Christ.

Now let's talk about how you can get to know Him better and begin to enjoy the Christian life.

How Do I Talk to God?
How Does He Talk to Me?

Some people view Christianity and living the Christian life as following a list of rules, rituals, and regulations. But that doesn't sound very exciting or enjoyable, does it? One reason people view Christianity this way is that they have failed to discover a clear difference between religious systems in the world and *biblical* Christianity.

Religion is society's way of doing something, such as working hard, going to church, being baptized, trying to keep the ten commandments, or being a good person, with the hope of somehow pleasing God, and being allowed into heaven. Unfortunately, because everyone has sinned (Rom. 3:23), even their best efforts fall short. Because the penalty for sin is death, everyone is destined for death—not just physical death but spiritual death (Rom. 6:23).

However, the good news is found in the message of Christ. (This is the difference between the religions of the world and biblical Christianity.) God says that Christ died for us, even though we are sinners (Rom. 5:8). God says we can be saved from the penalty of sin through simple faith, or trust, in Christ alone (Eph. 2:8–9).

Religion is our way of trying to reach God, but we will always come short. Christianity is God reaching down completely to us through the cross of Christ. When you place your trust in Christ, you enter into a relationship with Christ that God wants you to enjoy.

God intended the Christian life to be a relationship—a meaningful and fulfilling relationship. That is the reason 1 John 1:2–4 says of Christ, "The life was manifested, and we have seen and bear witness and proclaim to you the eternal life, which was with the Father and was manifested to us—what we have seen and heard we proclaim to you also, that you also may have fellowship with us; and indeed *our fellowship is with the Father, and with His Son Jesus Christ.* And these things we write, so that our joy may be made complete."

In any relationship, the more you communicate the closer you become. You became close to your best friend by talking and listening. It is no different when it comes to developing your relationship with God. When someone places his or her trust in Christ as Savior, God delights in communicating with them. That's what He wants to do with you. You need to let God speak to you, and you need to speak with God. How does this happen?

God Speaks to Us Through the Bible

Why should you let God speak to you through the Bible? That's a good question! A key section of the Scripture to study on this subject is 2 Timothy 3:16–17. Examine these verses carefully and see what you learn.

All Scripture is inspired by God and profitable for teaching, for reproof, for correction, for training in righteousness; that the man of God may be adequate, equipped for every good work.

1. Where did the Bible come from?

    _____

    The phrase, "All Scripture is inspired by God" means that the Bible comes from an amazing source—God Himself. Another verse, 2 Peter 1:21, helps to explain what this means. It says, "men moved by the Holy Spirit spoke from God." This means that God directed the human authors using their own personalities to write God's words without error.

2. What influence does the Bible have on Christians who read it?

    _____

    Scripture is "profitable for teaching, for reproof, for correction, for training in righteousness." What do these words mean? Let's look at each one.

    a. "profitable for *teaching*"
        The Bible teaches you what is true.

b. "profitable for *reproof*"
The Bible shows you where you are wrong.

c. "profitable for *correction*"
The Bible shows you how to correct your conduct.

d. "profitable for *training in righteousness*"
The Bible shows you how to develop proper habits.

3. What results come about in your life as you read the Bible?

a. The Bible is God's instrument for changing how you *think*.

b. The Bible is God's instrument for changing how you *live*.

God will help you take out of your life the things that should not be there, and will help put into your life what should be there. As your life changes and conforms to godly habits and thoughts, you will enjoy your relationship with Christ more and more.

4. If the Bible can do all of this for me, where do I start? There are five basic ways you can feed on the Scriptures:

a. *Hearing* stimulates your interest and gives you new insights.

b. *Reading* gives you an overall picture of biblical truth.

c. *Studying* enables you to discover principles to change your thoughts and conduct.

d. *Memorizing* makes principles you have learned available to you for everyday use.

e. *Meditating* encourages you to apply the Bible to your life.

As you grow in your discovery of the riches of Scripture and experience the satisfaction that comes from obeying God's principles, you will want to spend more and more time hearing, reading, studying, memorizing, and meditating.

Remember, God did not give you the Bible to simply satisfy your curiosity; He gave you the Scriptures to change the way you think and live!

5. How do you interact with what you read?

There are many approaches to Bible study. These suggestions will help you get started. However, before explaining how to do it, a few ideas about *when* and *where* to study the Word will help you.

a. *Make it a priority*—Study daily, preferably as you begin your day. You will discover that the business and events of everyday life can crowd out your Bible reading.

b. *Make it personal*—Study with the purpose of getting to know God better and of sensing God's direction and presence in your life.

c. *Make a place to do it*—Most people learn that their Bible study is more meaningful when they find a convenient, quiet place to study and reflect on the Scriptures.

d. *Make a plan*—As you begin your study, it will be helpful to follow a regular pattern.

   1) Start with one book of the Bible and read one chapter in that book each day for one month. Philippians is an excellent book to study first. When you finish with Philippians, go to the next book (Colossians), and do the same for one month.

   2) As you read, record your thoughts using the guide on the next page for each chapter in the Bible that you study.

   3) Pray about the things you read. The next section will give you further direction.

Philippians
Chapter 1

	What I Observe	How It Applies to Me
v. 1	*Paul and Timothy were servants of Christ.*	*I should see myself as a servant of Christ.*
v. 2	*Grace and peace come from God and Jesus Christ.*	*I should sense God's peace in my life.*
v. 3	*Paul thanked God when he thought of other Christians.*	*I can be thankful for Christians I know.*
v. 4		
v. 5		
v. 6		
v. 7		
v. 8		

Follow this procedure for each chapter of each book of the Bible that you study.

You Speak to God Through Prayer

Communication requires at least two people. It is important for you to let God speak to you through the Bible, but you also need to speak to God through prayer. Several questions may come to your mind.

1. What is prayer?

   Prayer is calling upon God and asking Him to work in your life or in the lives of others. In Matthew 6:9–13 (often called the Lord's Prayer), Jesus gives us a model of prayer. He emphasizes the importance of asking God to meet our needs and the needs of others, even though He reminds us, "Your Father knows the things you have need, before you ask Him" (Matt. 6:8). It is significant that four times in Matthew 6:5–7 Jesus equated this prayer with the concept of *asking* God for something.

2. If God knows my needs before I ask, then why ask? The answer seems to rest in the idea that prayer conveys an attitude of total dependence on God to meet our every need. Every prayer you express is a demonstration of faith (or dependence) on God to meet your needs physically, spiritually, emotionally, and mentally.

3. How do I talk to God in prayer?

   Pray as to a loving, caring *father*. Pray as to a sensitive, trusting *friend*. Philippians 4:6–7 can give you a good start in directing you in your prayers.

   > Be anxious for nothing, but in everything by prayer and supplication with thanksgiving let your requests be made known to God. And the peace of God, which surpasses all comprehension, shall guard your hearts and your minds in Christ Jesus.

   a. How many things in life does God want me to worry about?

   _____

God does not want you to go through life carrying the burden of worry and anxiety. *Be anxious for nothing.*

b. How many of the things that I worry about does God want me to pray about?

_____

But in everything by prayer and supplication. In every matter of concern God wants you to pray specifically. That is what the word *supplication* means.

c. In the midst of difficulties, what should my attitude be when I pray?

_____

God wants you to pray *with thanksgiving.* This sounds strange when you first think about it. In the midst of things that would bother you, God wants you to pray with a grateful heart. Why? When you trust God to allow only circumstances in your life for your own good, you can accept them and respond more appropriately.

d. What does God promise for those who follow these directions in their life?

_____

_____

The peace of God, which surpasses all comprehension will guard your hearts and minds in Christ Jesus. This means that God will guard or protect your heart—the center of your emotional being—as well as your mind—the center of your mental processes—through your relationship with Christ.

4. What do you do when your mind is distracted?

_____

_____

The Scriptures indicate that prayer can be hard work. It takes time and discipline to pray effectively without using "vain repetitions" which Jesus warned against in Matthew 6:7. It can be helpful to make a prayer list ahead of time and pray for each request. It is also wise to pray as you are directed by Scripture.

5. When and where do you pray?

   The Bible gives two answers to this question:

   a. Pray at a *regular* time and place.

   b. Pray *any* time at *any* place!

   Scripture indicates that Jesus did both, making prayer a regular part of His life, often beginning His day in prayer and meditation. Look up these verses in your New Testament and write down *when* and *where,* if stated, Jesus prayed.

   Mark 1:35 _____

   Mark 6:46 _____

   Luke 5:16 _____

   Luke 6:12 _____

   If prayer was this important to Jesus, imagine how important it is for each of us!

Conclusion

Remember that this chapter began by talking about Christianity as a relationship. You don't get close to God overnight. It is developed day by day, week by week, and month by month as you take time talking with Him and allowing Him to speak to you through His Word, the Bible.

The more you spend time with Him, the more you will discover that Christianity is not a matter of following a list of rules, rituals, and regulations. It is a growing, dynamic relationship with Jesus Christ.

As you grow in your Christian life, you will gain a new perspective on your relationships with people.

How Will My Relationships Change?

God never intended for you to live the Christian life alone. He knows that you need the encouragement and support that you can only receive from other Christians. When the Bible talks about this type of meaningful interaction with other Christians, it is often called *fellowship*.

What Is Christian Fellowship?

When the word "fellowship" is used in the New Testament, it includes the idea of association, close relationship, participation, and sharing. First Corinthians 1:9 says, "God is faithful, through whom you were called into fellowship with His Son, Jesus Christ our Lord." Notice that this verse says you have been brought into a close sharing relationship with God through Jesus Christ—a relationship that will make your life purposeful and meaningful. As Christians we can relate to each other in a way that encourages growth in our relationships with Christ.

That is what Scripture talks about in Hebrews 10:24–25: "And let us consider how to stimulate one another to love and good deeds, not forsaking our own assembling together, as is the habit of some, but encouraging one another; and all the more, as you see the day drawing near." Let's focus on a few thoughts in these verses.

1. To what actions does God ask Christians to *stimulate* or encourage each other in?

   _____

2. If you are going to obey God's command in this area, there is
   something you are told *not* to do. What is it?

   _____

   The phrase *not forsaking our own assembling together* is a
   command for you to meet regularly with other Christians.

What Is the Church?

Remember that the church is a group of Christians relating to each
other because of their common relationship to Christ. At the moment
you place your trust in Christ, you are immediately placed *into the
body of Christ,* which is the church, by means of God's Holy Spirit.

Please note that a group of Christians gathered together to obey
God's commands and fulfill His purposes (described later in this chapter) is what the Bible calls the *church.* Sometimes in the Bible, the
word *church* also refers to Christians all over the world, and at other
times it refers to a group of believers in one location—a local church.

Christ's instructions to His church are provided primarily in the New
Testament books of Romans through Revelation (though Revelation
4–22 deal with the future). It is these books, called "letters" or "epistles,"
that help you understand what the church is, how Christ relates to the
church, and how God wants Christians to relate to each other. When
you begin to understand these matters, you will have a better understanding of Christian fellowship and how it can help you spiritually.

1. What is the position of Christ to the church?

   Ephesians 1:22–23 says, "And He [God] put all things in sub-
   jection under His feet, and gave Him as head over all things to
   the church, which is His body, the fullness of Him who fills all
   in all."

   Notice it says that Christ is *head over all things to the church.*
   This means that you are to receive direction and instruction
   from Christ. In the last chapter you saw how God directs you
   through His Word, the Bible.

2. What is the position of Christians in the church?

"For just as we have many members in one body and all the members do not have the same function, so we, who are many, are one body in Christ, and individually members one of another" (Romans 12:4–5).

"For even as the body is one and yet has many members, and all the members of the body, though they are many, are one body, so also is Christ. . . . But now there are many members, but one body. . . . that there should be no division in the body, but that the members should have the same care for one another" (1 Corinthians 12:12, 20, 25).

What does this tell us about the body of Christ and the members in the body?

_____

_____

_____

Although there is one body, it has *many members*. Why? Read the verses again.

_____

_____

_____

There should be no division in the body. The members should care for one another. In other words, when the members of Christ's body—called the church—relate to each other the way God wants, they will meet each other's needs and fulfill God's purposes for the church on this earth.

3. What are the purposes and functions of the church?

To answer this important question thoroughly, you would have to read the entire New Testament. Here is a summary of the

major purposes and functions that God desires for His church—
the members of His body.

- Introduce non-Christians to Christ and help them to follow Him (Matt. 28:19–20).
- Baptize new Christians (Matt. 28:19–20).
- Teach Christians the Scriptures (Acts 2:42).
- Offer worship and praise to God (Rom. 15:5–6).
- Participate in the Lord's Supper or communion (1 Cor. 11:23–33).
- Exercise spiritual gifts to encourage Christians (1 Cor. 12:4–31).
- Correct and discipline Christians who are disobeying God (Matt. 5:22–24; 18:15–17).
- Encourage Christians to become mature followers of Christ (Eph. 4:11–16).
- Encourage Christians to live a holy life before non-Christians (Phil. 2:15–16).
- Encourage Christians in their faith (Heb. 3:13; 10:24–25).
- Meet the needs of Christians (Gal. 6:9–10).
- Give financially to promote God's work (1 Cor. 16:1–2; 2 Cor. 9:6–8).
- Promote purity of doctrine, or teaching (Rom. 16:17).
- Bring glory to God (1 Cor. 10:31).
- Pray for Christians and non-Christians (Acts 2:42).

How Can I Find a Good Church?

Depending on where you live, it may take some time to find a good church. A "good church" involves a group of believers meeting regularly together to fulfill the purposes and functions mentioned above.
A solid church also meets these guidelines:

1. The church is committed to introducing non-Christians to salvation through faith in Christ, and then helping them to grow spiritually (Matt. 28:19–20).
2. The church believes that a person receives the free gift of eternal life through faith, or trust, in Christ alone as their only way to heaven (John 3:16, 3:36; 5:24; 6:47; 14:6; 20:30–31).

3. The people of the church display genuine love for each other (John 13:34).
4. The leaders of the church are spiritually mature in their relationship with Christ and others (1 Tim. 3:1–13).
5. The church believes that the Bible is the accurate, authoritative Word of God; designed to direct us in our faith and life so we may be equipped for every good work (2 Tim. 3:16–17).
6. The believers come together to love and encourage each other to please God in their daily lives (Heb. 10:24–25).

When you find a good church and attend regularly, you are meeting with the people God wants you to *fellowship* with. Don't go simply to receive but to give. Don't go simply to give but to receive. That is what fellowship is all about.

What's Necessary for Fellowship?

How can a new believer understand and experience *fellowship* in the church?

1. You must be living in obedience to Christ.

   Notice what 1 John 1:5–7 says concerning this: "And this is the message we have heard from Him and announce to you, that God is light, and in Him there is no darkness at all. If we say that we have fellowship with Him and yet walk in the darkness [that is, disobedience], we lie and do not practice the truth; but if we walk in the light as He Himself is in the light, we have fellowship with one another, and the blood of Jesus His Son cleanses us from all sin."

   This means that you know you are a Christian, or a *believer* in Jesus Christ, and you are living in obedience to Christ's commandments in the Scriptures.

2. You must be showing kindness to Christians in the church.

   Galatians 6:10 says, "So then, while we have opportunity, let us do good to all men, and especially to those who are of the household of the faith."

Who are you to serve by doing good?

_____

Who are you to *especially* serve by doing good?

_____

The phrase *those who are of the household of the faith* is a reference to members of Christ's body, the church.

Before you can experience Christian fellowship, you must be living in obedience to Christ and live with other Christians the way Scripture asks.

What's My Part?

We can answer this question by considering two things that God desires for every Christian.

1. Christians should obey the specific commands in the *one another* passages in Scripture. Please note that the phrase *one another* appears many times in the New Testament. Carefully read and reflect on each of the following passages.

    *   Love one another (John 13:34; 15:12, 17).
    *   Be devoted to one another (Rom. 12:10).
    *   Be of the same mind toward one another (Rom. 12:16; 15:5).
    *   Do not judge one another (Rom. 14:13).
    *   Build up one another (Rom. 14:19).
    *   Accept one another (Rom. 15:7).
    *   Admonish one another (Rom. 15:14).
    *   Greet one another warmly (1 Cor. 16:20).
    *   Have the same care for one another (1 Cor. 12:25).
    *   Serve one another (Gal. 5:13).
    *   Don't challenge or envy one another (Gal. 5:26).
    *   Bear one another's burdens (Gal. 6:2).
    *   Show forbearance to one another (Eph. 4:2).
    *   Be kind to one another (Eph. 4:32).
    *   Submit to one another (Eph. 5:21).

- Regard one another as more important than yourself (Phil. 2:3).
- Do not lie to one another (Col. 3:9).
- Forbear and forgive one another (Col. 3:13).
- Comfort one another (1 Thess. 4:18; 5:11).
- Seek that which is good for one another (1 Thess. 5:15).
- Encourage one another to love and good deeds (Heb. 10:24).
- Do not speak evil of one another (James 4:11).
- Do not complain about one another (James 5:9).
- Confess your sins to one another (James 5:16).
- Pray for one another (James 5:16).
- Show hospitality to one another (1 Peter 4:9).

2. Christians should discover and exercise their spiritual gifts.

What are spiritual gifts? First Peter 4:10 says, "As each one has received a *special gift*, employ it in serving one another, as good stewards of the manifold grace of God."

What has each Christian received?

_____

What is each Christian to do with this gift?

_____

_____

Each believer in Christ has been given at least one spiritual gift to encourage and minister to other Christians in the church.

What Are Spiritual Gifts?

There are three places in the New Testament where spiritual gifts are listed. It is clear that God distributes certain gifts to Christians for specific reasons.

There are thirteen gifts clearly in use in the church today. There are four foundational gifts that served the church while it was in its early stages. When the church reached a point of relative maturity, these gifts were no longer needed (1 Cor. 13:8, Eph. 2:20).

The four signifying or "sign" gifts were related to the foundational gifts. Many Bible teachers believe that these gifts served to confirm or verify the message of the apostles and died out with the apostolic era (1 Cor. 13:8; 2 Cor. 12:12; Heb. 2:3–4).

Gifts Present Today

1. Service (Rom. 12:7)
2. Teaching (Rom. 12:7)
3. Exhortation (Rom. 12:8)
4. Giving (Rom. 12:8)
5. Ruling (Rom. 12:8)
6. Mercy (Rom. 12:8)
7. Wisdom (1 Cor. 12:8)
8. Faith (1 Cor. 12:9)
9. Discernment (1 Cor. 12:10)
10. Administration (1 Cor. 12:28)
11. Helps (1 Cor. 12:28)
12. Pastoring (Eph. 4:11)
13. Evangelism (Eph. 4:11)

Foundational Gifts

14. Apostleship (1 Cor. 12:28–29; Eph. 4:11)
15. Prophet (1 Cor. 12:28–29; Eph. 4:11)
16. Prophecy (Rom. 12:6; 1 Cor. 12:10)
17. Knowledge (1 Cor. 12:8)

Sign Gifts

18. Healing (1 Cor. 12:9, 28, 30)
19. Miracles (1 Cor. 12:10, 28–29)
20. Tongues (1 Cor. 12:10, 28, 30)
21. Interpretation of tongues (1 Cor. 12:10)

How do I discover my spiritual gift and fulfill the *one another* commands? This is much simpler than you might think.

1. Develop your personal relationship with Christ.

   Simply spend time with the Lord by studying the Bible and praying. As you do, you will maintain a balanced and proper relationship with Christ.

2. Spend time serving other Christians.

   As you seek to relate to other members of the body, you will seek ways to serve them. Do whatever you can to help. As you serve, godly men and women will recognize areas of ministry where God has given you special ability, and they will encourage you in those areas of service.

   As you serve and encourage others, they will also encourage you. You will draw closer to Christ and build up one another in the faith.

Conclusion

God never intended for you to live the Christian life alone. He knows that you need the support and encouragement of others who, like you, have placed their trust in Christ.

When you are fellowshipping with Christ and properly related to other believers in Christ, you will experience *Christian fellowship*, which we can now define as:

> *Christian fellowship is the mutual exchange of the benefits of our relationships with Christ.*

If you and I are maintaining a close walk with Christ, when we get together, we should encourage each other in our Christian life. You will benefit from my relationship with Christ, and I will benefit from your relationship with Christ.

What Does It Mean to Follow Christ?

The excitement you have begun to experience in the Christian life has only started. It can grow and deepen with time. That is why Jesus said in John 10:10, "I came that they might have life, and might have it abundantly."

However, the Scriptures are clear that an abundant life does not happen automatically. It is only available to those Christians who continue to grow in their walk with Christ. The abundant life is available to those who grow as *disciples*. What is a disciple? What does being a disciple of Jesus involve? What are the benefits?

What Is a Disciple?

The word *disciple* in the New Testament simply means "a pupil" or "learner." A *disciple* is a student and follower of someone who assumes the position of their teacher. In the New Testament we have a record of people who were *followers* and *learners* of particular individuals including:

- disciples of John the Baptist (Matt. 9:14)
- disciples of Jesus Christ (Mark 2:15)
- disciples of Moses (John 9:28)
- disciples of the apostle Paul (Acts 9:25)

Please note something very important: A person can be a *disciple* of someone other than Christ and be a non-Christian. A person can be a disciple of Jesus—in the sense that he or she is learning about Him— and still not be a Christian (because he or she has not trusted Christ as their Savior). And it may seem surprising, but a person can be a believer in Christ—a true Christian—but stop *growing* as a disciple!

You can now understand and appreciate why the New Testament makes a distinction between *entering* the Christian life and *living* the Christian life. You *enter* the Christian life at one point in time by trusting Christ alone to pay for your sin. Everything you do from that point on provides the opportunity for you to *live* the Christian life by growing in your relationship with Christ.

In this chapter you will learn what is involved in becoming a disciple of Jesus Christ in its fullest, richest sense—someone who is a believer in Christ and *continues* to follow and live for Him—what we will call a *growing disciple.*

Where Do I Begin?

Discipleship begins by recognizing that *God wants you to live a life that says "thank you" for what He has given you in Christ.* Once you trust Christ, everything you do from that point on should represent and demonstrate a "thank you" for what Christ has done for you. Here's a helpful illustration:

Let's suppose you were in the hospital dying of a rare disease. I was the one doctor who knew how to cure it, and I forever cured you of that disease.

Now suppose that a few years later I say to you, "I need some help repairing my home; could you give me some help?" You reply, "No, I'm too busy. Get someone else." Is your life still saved? Sure, but that's a terrible way to say "thank you." In the same way, when you trust Christ, you are forever saved. Everything you do from that point on is a "thank you." If a believer does not live for Christ, it doesn't change his or her salvation, but since the way he or she lives is dishonoring to God, it is a poor way to say "thank you."

How do you live a life that says "thank you"?

1. Understand what Romans 12:1–2 says to you:

    "I urge you therefore, brethren, by the mercies of God, to present your bodies a living and holy sacrifice, acceptable to

God, which is your spiritual service of worship. And do not be conformed to this world, but be transformed by the renewing of your mind, that you may prove what the will of God is, that which is good and acceptable and perfect."

a. How would you describe the tone of these verses?

_____

The apostle Paul says, *I urge you!* He has very strong feelings about these instructions.

b. Who is Paul talking to in this passage?

_____

Notice that he is talking to *brethren*. These are people who have placed their trust in Christ. They are Christians; they are on their way to heaven.

c. On what basis does Paul ask these things?

_____

He urges them to respond based on *the mercies of God*. God has richly displayed His mercy toward every person who trusts Christ's death and resurrection to pay the penalty for their sin. Their sins are forgiven, they are unconditionally accepted through Christ, they have the assurance of heaven, and much more!

d. What specifically does Paul ask you to do?

_____

_____

He asks you *to present your bodies a living and holy sacrifice, acceptable to God, which is your spiritual service of worship*. If God has your body, He has all of you—your mind, your heart, your hands, your feet, your eyes. In other words, He asks you to make yourself completely available to Him to serve Him, worship Him, and obey Him. Observe that God is saying that what we do with our daily life is a way to honor and worship Him.

e. What does this idea of presenting yourself require?

_____

_____

God says, *Do not be conformed to this world.* The word *world* in the Bible often refers to the world system—values and ideas that are opposed to what is right and good in the sight of God. That is why God tells us in 1 John 2:15–16, "Do not love the world, nor the things in the world. If anyone loves the world, the love of the Father is not in him. For all that is in the world, *the lust of the flesh* and *the lust of the eyes* and *the boastful pride of life*, is not from the Father, but is from the world." God does not want us to embrace the ideas and values that the world presents to us.

God also says, *be transformed by the renewing of your mind.* We can be different people when we look at life through His eyes. If we are to live holy lives, then we must think holy thoughts. We must think differently than we used to!

f. Is all of this really worth it? Put the answer found in verse 2 in your own words.

_____

_____

_____

_____

He continues, *that you may prove what the will of God is, that which is good and acceptable and perfect.* As we allow God to change our thinking—when we respond in obedience—it changes our habits. When we change the way we live, we experience the benefits and blessings of living by God's principles. Over a period of time we come to recognize that God's will—what He desires for us—is *good*, and *acceptable*. More than that, it is *perfect*.

2. Obey the commands in Romans 12:1–2.

Let's review what God wants you to do as a way of saying "thank you" after you become a Christian.

  a. Make an initial, decisive act of presenting yourself to God to obey Him and follow Him.

  b. Allow God to continue to transform your mind—or change the way you think.

  c. Separate yourself from the "world system" and its values.

  d. Submit in obedience to God's will.

3. Obey Christ's command to be baptized as a Christian.

In Matthew 28:19–20 two steps are involved in becoming a growing disciple of Christ: First, baptism assumes that you have already put your trust in Christ and for that reason are obeying His command to be baptized (v. 19). Second, the outworking or result of that one-time decision is learning how to obey all that Christ commanded (v. 20). These two phases are similar to Romans 12:1–2 where you make a decision to present your bodies to God. What is the outworking or result? You continue to be transformed by the renewing of your mind.

  a. In the New Testament those who believed in Christ were baptized (Acts 2:41; 8:12, 36–38; 16:14–15, 30–33; 18:8).

  b. Baptism does not save you. It identifies you as a believer with Christ in His death and resurrection and portrays that you may now "walk in newness of life" (Rom. 6:3–5).

  c. Baptism serves as a public testimony and act of obedience to Christ. As the first major act of obedience to Christ, it is the biblical way to tell others, "I belong to Christ and from this point on, by God's power, intend to live in obedience to Him" (Matt. 28:19–20).

4. Continue to grow as a disciple.

What Characterizes a Growing Disciple?

Over a period of time, as you continue to respond in obedience to what you learn from the Scriptures, you will begin to reflect the characteristics of a *growing disciple* of Christ in its fullest and richest sense. The Bible often uses the term *disciple* to refer to someone who is *a believer in Christ* who lives in obedience to Him. The New Testament points to at least seven characteristics of this growing disciple.

1. A growing disciple progresses from a point of mere curiosity about Christ to the point where he or she is convinced that only through trust in Christ alone can one have eternal life (John 6:64–68).

2. A growing disciple will continue to study God's Word (John 8:31–32).

3. A growing disciple will display a sacrificial love for other believers (John 13:34–35).

4. A growing disciple will display a fruitful, obedient life (John 15:1–16, especially v. 8).

5. A growing disciple is consistent in prayer (Luke 11:1–10).

6. A growing disciple will be committed to bringing other people to faith in Christ and helping them to become mature followers of Christ (Matt. 28:19–20).

7. A growing disciple of Jesus Christ will be totally committed to obeying God's will for his or her life, even though it is very costly (Luke 14:25–33).

What Are the Benefits?

There are many benefits to responding in obedience to God's command to live as a growing disciple. You could summarize all of the benefits in two major points.

1. Living as a *growing disciple* brings blessing and contentment throughout our life on this earth.

   a. Jesus said in John 10:10, "I came that they might have life, and might have it abundantly."

   b. Obedience to God's Word frees us from the bondage of sin. John 8:31–32 says, "Jesus therefore was saying to those Jews who had believed in Him, 'If you abide in My word, then you are truly disciples of Mine; and you shall know the truth, and the truth shall make you free.'"

   c. A favorable response to God's discipline in life has its rewards. So Hebrews 12:11 says, "All discipline for the moment seems not to be joyful, but sorrowful; yet to those who have been trained by it, afterwards it yields the peaceful fruit of righteousness."

2. Living as a *growing disciple* brings the blessing of eternal reward that God promises for those who faithfully obey and serve Him.

   a. Every Christian will be rewarded for the quality of their obedience and service to Christ. When we are disobedient to Christ it results in loss of eternal *reward* (not loss of our salvation). That is why 1 Corinthians 3:11–15 says,

   "For no man can lay a foundation other than the one which is laid, which is [faith in] Jesus Christ. Now if any man builds upon the foundation with gold, silver, precious stones [worthy deeds], wood, hay, straw [unworthy deeds], each man's work will become evident; for the day will show it, because it is to be revealed with fire; and the fire itself will test the quality of each man's work. If any man's work which he has built upon remains [after testing], he shall receive a reward. If any man's work is burned up, he shall suffer loss [of reward]; but he himself will be saved, yet so as through fire."

   b. Christians who sacrifice to serve and obey Christ will have a special place of reward in Christ's coming kingdom. Revelation 22:12 says, "Behold, I am coming quickly, and My reward is with Me, to render to every man according to what he has done."

Conclusion

The life of a growing disciple is not easy, but it is the best life. *Salvation* through Christ is free, *discipleship* is costly. *Entering* the Christian life is receiving a free gift by trusting Christ; *living* the Christian life as a growing disciple involves work. How will you respond to God's challenge to you to follow Christ as His disciple?

Here is a sample prayer you could use to express your dedication to God:

Dear God, I have already done what you desire every person to do—trust Christ alone as my only way to heaven. Now I understand more than ever why you don't just want me to *enter* the Christian life, you want me to *live* the Christian life. You want me to follow You and grow as Your disciple.

Instead of trying to do things my way, and running my own life, I want to obey you and follow You. More than that, I want to continue to learn from You. I want to be Your disciple in the fullest and richest sense.

Right now, God, I am using this prayer as an expression of my commitment to You. Help me from this day forward to live the type of life as a Christian that says "thank you" for what you have given me in Jesus Christ. In Jesus' name, amen.

How Do I Maintain a Close Relationship with Christ?

Living as a growing disciple of Jesus requires your commitment to follow through on some daily disciplines. In this chapter, you will look at five basic areas involved in maintaining a close walk with Christ. The first two have already been discussed in the second chapter. More time will be given to those areas that have not yet been discussed.

What are these areas that describe how to maintain a close relationship with Christ as a growing disciple?

Communicate with God Daily

Take time each day to get to know God better by reading the Bible and praying (2 Tim. 3:16–17; Phil. 4:6–7). As was discussed in the second chapter, communication between you and God is essential for spiritual growth.

Fellowship with Other Christians

By meeting regularly with other believers, you can encourage them and they can encourage you (Heb. 10:24–25). Review the material in chapter three, and it will remind you of how important it is for you to experience and benefit from genuine Christian fellowship.

Confess Sin Daily

The word "confess" means to admit, or agree with God where you have violated His commands and principles. This would seem to present a problem. If God is sinless and does not tolerate sin in His presence, what hope is there for you when you sin? Wouldn't you do better to pretend you didn't sin? First John 1:8–9 give us the answer. Notice what we can learn from these verses:

1. God says that all Christians sin; don't try to hide your sins from Him.

   "If we say that we have no sin, we are deceiving ourselves, and the truth is not in us" (1 John 1:8).

2. God says that when we confess our sins to Him, He forgives us for those sins.

   "If we confess our sins, He is faithful and righteous to forgive us our sins. . . ." (1 John 1:9).

3. God says that when we confess our sins to Him that He forgives us for *all* of our sins.

   "If we confess our sins, He is faithful and righteous to forgive us our sins and to cleanse us from all unrighteousness" (1 John 1:9).

   When we confess known sin, notice that God even forgives unknown sin. Because God is perfect, we can only maintain a closeness with Him when we acknowledge that we have been imperfect, which will be quite often! We admit our failures when we confess our sins to God.

Trust Through Trials

1. What is a trial?

   A trial is anything that tests your faith or confidence in God. The Bible describes various types of trials that Christians will encounter:

   a. Difficulties allowed by God to test our faith (Heb. 11:17)

b. Some form of persecution (1 Peter 2:19–21)

c. Suffering of various forms (1 Peter 4:12–16)

d. Assault by our spiritual enemy, Satan (1 Peter 5:8–10)

2. If God loves me and cares about me, why would He allow trials and difficulties to come into my life?

As you will soon see, trials are designed to help you, not hurt you. When you learn to look at them from God's perspective, and respond as God desires, you'll have the answer.

3. How does God want me to respond to trials?

Although there are many sections of Scripture that can help you learn how to respond to trials, we are going to focus on a key paragraph in James 1:2–4. Notice what it says:

"Consider it all joy, my brethren, when you encounter various trials, knowing that the testing of your faith produces endurance. And let endurance have its perfect result, that you may be perfect and complete, lacking in nothing" (v. 4).

a. How does God want you to respond when faced with trials?

_____

He wants us to consider it all joy. We can consider difficulties joyous because of the outcome or result they bring in our lives.

b. How are trials a normal part of life?

_____

When we encounter various trials, God wants us to understand that trials and difficulties are part of life. He does not say "if you encounter various trials," He says "when." They are inevitable for every Christian.

   c. How does God describe a trial?

      _____

      He refers to a trial as a testing of your *faith*. A trial is any-thing that tests your faith, or confidence, in God and your desire to respond in a way that would please and honor Him. By their very nature, trials will challenge and tempt you to respond in a way that would *not* honor God.

   d. What can a testing of your faith produce?

      _____

      God says that trials can produce endurance. Endurance re-fers to the type of mental attitude that perseveres under pres-sure and difficulty. This attitude is the foundation for a proper response to trials.

   e. What is the result of maintaining an attitude of endurance in the midst of trials?

      _____

      _____

      Endurance can have its *perfect result, that you may be perfect and complete, lacking in nothing.* These statements refer to the type of Christian character that honors God. It refers to having attitudes, conduct, and conversations that are pleasing to God and display a life of good works. Through the strength God supplies, recognize that God intends for these trials to draw you closer to Him and help you develop a mature Christian character.

Flee from Temptation

  1. What is a temptation?

      The word *temptation* comes from the same Greek word for trial because both involve the testing of our faith.

2. How does a temptation differ from a trial?

A trial it is a test that God allows. It is designed to develop our character. A temptation refers to an invitation to do something sinful. When God is the source of the test, there is no encouragement to do something sinful. However, our sinful bodies (often called "the flesh" in Scripture) or Satan, himself may enter in and influence us to want to do something sinful. Our flesh is enticed and wants us to sin. God wants us to strengthen our faith; Satan wants us to fail.

3. What Scripture can help me understand the difference between a trial and a temptation?

James 1:13–14 says, "Let no one say when he is tempted, 'I am being tempted by God,' for God cannot be tempted by evil, and He Himself does not tempt any one. But each one is tempted when he is carried away and enticed by his own lust."

Verse 13 clearly states that God is not the *source* of temptation. Although He will *allow* trials to strengthen us and develop our character, there is never a temptation from God to do wrong. Verse 14 explains that temptation comes from desires within us as we are enticed by our own lust.

4. How can I overcome temptations?

The Bible has much to say about how we can confront and overcome temptations. A key verse is 1 Corinthians 10:13.

"No temptation has overtaken you but such as is common to man; and God is faithful, who will not allow you to be tempted beyond what you are able, but with the temptation will provide the way of escape also, that you may be able to endure it."

a. How many people struggle with temptation?

_____

The verse says that temptations are common to everyone. You are not alone!

b. How will God help us handle the temptation?

_____

_____

God is faithful, who will not allow you to be tempted beyond what you are able. God will limit the temptation to what you can endure. He will never allow you to face more than what you can handle with His help.

c. How else will God help us?

_____

_____

God will provide the way of escape from the temptation. He will make sure that you have the resources and ability to stand up against temptation. But notice that this may sometimes include the challenge of you enduring the temptation.

Conclusion

To review, you maintain a close relationship with Christ as you:

- Communicate with God daily

- Fellowship with other Christians

- Confess sin daily

- Trust through trials

- Flee from temptation

How Do I Share Christ with Others?

Someone who cared about you told you about the most important person you could ever meet—Jesus Christ! Now that you know Christ, God wants you to tell others about Him. God wants you to live for people, not material things. The chapters dealing with fellowship and discipleship have made that clear already. An integral part of discipleship is telling others about Christ. The first thing Jesus said to His disciples was recorded for us in Matthew 4:18–19:

> And walking by the Sea of Galilee, He saw two brothers, Simon who was called Peter, and Andrew his brother, casting a net into the sea; for they were fishermen. And He said to them, "Follow Me," and I will make you fishers of men.

From the very beginning, Jesus called people to be His disciples who would tell others of the need to place their faith in Christ. Once these people came to faith in Christ, His disciples would help these new Christians grow so they could become mature followers of Christ. (See Rom. 12:1–2; Matt. 28:19–20.)

In this chapter we want to talk about you sharing Christ with somebody else. When we tell others about Christ we are doing *evangelism*. What is it and how do we do it?

What Is Evangelism?

Evangelism comes from a Greek word that means "good news." Although used in several different ways in the Bible, the word also refers to the good news about Christ. The Good News, or *Gospel,* is what God has done for us through Jesus Christ.

How to Share Christ

1. You must clearly understand the biblical message God wants you to proclaim to non-Christians.

    a. Notice the verbs of the message in 1 Corinthians 15:3–5.

        Christ died for our sins according to the Scriptures, and that He was buried, and that He was raised on the third day according to the Scriptures, and that He appeared.

    b. Christ's burial is proof that He died. The fact that Christ appeared is proof that He was raised.

    c. Therefore, on the basis of this paragraph, the gospel is simply: Christ died for our *sins and rose from the dead.*

    d. Don't confuse what God has made so clear. Simply explain the Gospel!

2. Be clear on how God asks the non-Christian to respond to that message.

    Over and over again the New Testament asks people to trust Christ alone as their only way to heaven. The Gospel of John tells us how we can know we are going to heaven. John gives us his purpose for writing in John 20:30–31. He stresses trust by using the word *believe* ninety-eight times in the book!

3. You must have a clear way to present the message.

    The simple bad news/good news approach we looked at earlier is a method you should study carefully. It will enable you to present the gospel clearly and concisely. You will find it easy to remember, and you will discover that the bad news/good news approach is something nonbelievers can easily identify with. Review this outline and refer to pages 11–14 to learn the complete presentation.

The Bad News

You are a sinner: "For all have sinned and fall short of the glory of God" (Rom. 3:23).

The penalty for sin is death: "For the wages of sin is death" (Rom. 6:23).

The Good News

Christ died for you: "But God demonstrates His own love toward us, in that while we were still sinners, Christ died for us" (Rom. 5:8).

You can be saved through faith: "For by grace you have been saved through faith; and that not of yourselves, it is the *gift* of God; not as a result of works, that no one should boast" (Eph. 2:8–9).

4. Ask them to respond to the message.

   a. "Is there anything keeping you from trusting Christ?"

      If the person seems hesitant, take a piece of paper and number from one to five on the left hand side. Ask the individual to list a few things that he or she feels are keeping him or her from trusting Christ. Answer each objection to the best of your ability.

      Remember that only the Holy Spirit can bring someone to Christ. However, you can help them think through what is keeping them from trusting Christ.

   b. When they are ready ask, "Would you like to pray and tell God that you are trusting His Son as your Savior?"

      I ask the other person to tell me how I could become a

Christian to make certain that he or she understands it. If
they do, I then do one of two things. I either lead him or her
in prayer or have them pray. Before doing either, make certain that they understand that saying a prayer has never saved
anyone. Prayer is only the means by which one can tell
God that they've trusted Jesus Christ as their Savior.

  c. Have them express their faith in Christ using this prayer:
  "Dear God, I come to You now. I know that I am a sinner.
  Nothing I am or do makes me deserving of heaven. I believe
  Jesus Christ died for me and rose from the grave. I trust Jesus
  Christ alone as my Savior. Thank you for the forgiveness
  and everlasting life I now have. In Jesus' name. Amen."

5. Immediately cover assurance of salvation with them as explained on pages 14–16.

Effective Evangelism

1. Pray for your evangelistic efforts. Here are a few key areas
   Scripture asks you to pray for:

   a. Pray for opportunities (Col. 4:3).

   b. Pray for courage to proclaim the message clearly (Acts
      4:29–31).

   c. Pray for salvation—that individuals will respond by trust-
      ing Christ alone as their Savior (1 Tim. 2:1–8).

2. Display wisdom in your conduct and conversation. Matthew
   10:16 says, "Behold, I send you out as sheep in the midst of
   wolves; therefore be shrewd as serpents, and innocent as
   doves." What does that involve?

   Wisdom in evangelism can be summed up as common sense
   combined with a gracious spirit. In Colossians 4:5–6 God in-
   structs us to relate to nonbelievers with wisdom in our conduct and conversation with them. How do you do that?

_____

_____

_____

You can display wisdom by tactfully turning conversations to spiritual things. In other words, be sensitive to the person's openness to the message and the work of God's Spirit in preparing him or her to respond to the message (John 16:8–11).

3. Here is a strategy that will help you direct the conversation and discern the person's interest in spiritual matters.

   a. Create a casual and comfortable atmosphere. Simply begin conversing about subjects they are comfortable talking about.

   b. Give your mind the freedom to think. There is no one way to turn a conversation to spiritual things.

   c. Ask questions that gradually move the conversation from secular to spiritual subjects. How? Talk about three areas in which they are knowledgeable and give your mind the freedom to think. Ask about their:

      1) Family—parents, children, etc.
      2) Job—What do they do? What do they like or dislike about their vocation?
      3) Background—Where are they from? What is their educational background? Do they have special interests?

   d. If they open up to you as a person, assume that it is an opportunity to talk about spiritual things. You may want to ask:

      1) "Are you interested in spiritual things?"
      2) "You hear more and more people talk about Christ or Christianity. Who do you think Christ is?"

e. Ask questions that enable you to discern their interest and obtain their permission to present the gospel. It is very helpful to ask (in this order):

1) "May I ask you a more personal question?"
2) "Have you come to the place in your spiritual life where you know you will go to heaven, or are you somewhere along the way?"
3) "If you were to die and stand before God and He asked you, 'Why should I let you into heaven?' what would you tell Him?"
4) "Has anyone ever taken a Bible and shown you how you can know you will go to heaven? May I?"

f. Present the gospel.

Use the bad news/good news approach that was explained earlier. Review it until you can present it comfortably and confidently.

Planting Seeds

As you turn conversations to spiritual things and seek to talk to others about Christ, you will learn two facts.

1. People respond *differently* to the gospel. God wants everyone to come to faith in Christ (1 Tim. 2:4). God has prepared people to respond (John 4:35). In the process of evangelizing, we will find people at different stages of spiritual readiness. Recognize that God may use us to do the "sowing" for some and the "reaping" for others (John 4:36–38).

2. God does not require us to be *fruitful* in evangelism. God asks us, as His disciples, to be *faithful* in sharing the message.

Evangelism is sharing the Good News of Christ with the intent of seeing the person trust Christ. Whether or not the person comes to Christ is God's responsibility. God is asking you to bring the message to the lost, not to bring the lost to Christ (John 6:44).

Conclusion

God wants you to spend time with non-Christians so you can influence them for Christ. The more you grow in your walk with Christ, and the more time you spend with non-Christians, the more you will develop your skills in talking to them about Christ. The more you *do* it, the more you will learn *how* to do it. As you grow spiritually, you will be able to introduce others to Christ and then help them grow spiritually. You will reproduce in the lives of others what God has done in your life—help you live as a growing disciple.

As God uses you to reach others for Christ, remember this challenging thought:

> When I get to that beautiful city,
> and the saints all around me appear,
> I hope somebody comes up and says,
> "You're the one who invited me here."

EvanTell, Inc. is an association committed to a clear presentation of the gospel through a careful study of the Scripture. Its three main activities are:

CONFERENCES TO REACH
Operation Friendship is a single church outreach featuring a Saturday night outreach dinner and a Sunday morning outreach service, both directed toward non-Christians. A mini-seminar for believers follows on Sunday evening addressing how to overcome major struggles in evangelism.

EvanTell also offers a multi-church conference designed to impact an entire community for Christ.

SEMINARS TO TEACH
The popular *You Can Tell It!* seminar, taught by an approved instructor, helps believers overcome their two greatest worries in evangelism—fear of others and not knowing how to present the gospel.

The *You Can Preach It!* seminar gives thorough and practical instruction in developing biblical, evangelistic messages relevant to non-Christians.

MATERIALS TO EQUIP
Books, booklets, cassettes, videos, and an extensive training program prepare and strengthen believers for their ministry of evangelism.

9212 Markville Drive
Dallas, Texas 75243
972-690-3624

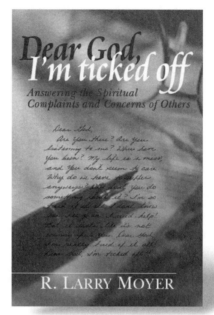

0-8254-3175-1   112 pp.

Dear God, I'm Ticked Off

Answering the Spiritual Complaints and Concerns of Others

by R. Larry Moyer

If a non-Christian or a disheartened Christian wrote an honest letter to God, what might it say? And what might God say in response? These two questions form the basis for Larry Moyer's honest and heart-touching series of letters addressed to God and the biblically based responses.

Some of the questions addressed include: Is God good? How could a loving God kill His own Son? Is the Bible reliable? How do I know who's right? What about my loved ones who have died? How can a loving God send me to hell? Will going to church get me to heaven? Why is the church full of hypocrites? Why didn't God come thRough for me in my crisis? Will God make me be a missionary? Why isn't life fair?

0-8254-3177-8   272 pp.

Free and Clear
Understanding and Communicating God's Offer of Eternal Life
by R. Larry Moyer

This handbook will lead believers step-by-step into a thorough understanding of the Gospel message, its biblical terminology and concepts. Group discussion questions are included at the end of each chapter.

"This book is for any pastor or layperson who takes the Great Commission seriously.... I think you'll come away with a fresh appreciation for the salvation we have in Christ, and a renewed desire to present the gospel to others." —Luis Palau

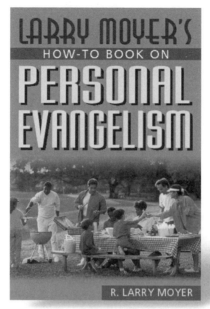

0-8254-3179-4   128 pp.

Larry Moyer's How-To Book on Personal Evangelism
by R. Larry Moyer

"I can't share the Gospel. I'm afraid I'll say something wrong—that is, if I knew what to say to begin with!" Have you ever found yourself thinking this? Larry Moyer draws from his twenty-five years of experience in evangelism to introduce readers to the exciting reality that believers *can* learn how to share the Gospel with others—confidently.

Even if you think evangelism isn't for you, this step-by-step resource shows you how to start and nurture an evangelistic lifestyle.

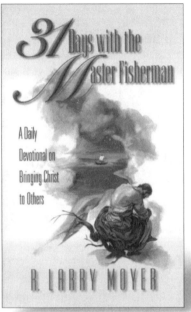

0-8254-3178-6   96 pp.

Thirty-One Days with the Master Fisherman
A Daily Devotional on Bringing Christ to Others
by R. Larry Moyer

It has been well said that many things are better caught than taught. This book encourages readers to spend time in reflection and meditation on the subjects of discipleship and evangelism. As we consider the things closest to Jesus' heart, we will catch His vision for sharing the Good News.

Written in a one-month, daily devotional format, this book is designed to encourage all believers to join in the Great Commission, to share the Good News, and to improve each person's skills in the greatest fishing expedition of all times!